The Garden Gnome Book

an illustrated history

by Marcus B. Mennes

QUIRK BOOKS

PHILADELPHIA

ISBN-10: 1-59474-010-0
ISBN-13: 978-1-59474-010-7

Manufactured in China

Gnome & Garden: A Gnovelty Kit is produced by
becker&mayer!, Ltd., Bellevue, Washington
www.beckermayer.com

Design by Joanna Price
Edited by Adrienne Wiley
Image Research by Shayna Ian
Production Coordination by Cindy Lashley

Distributed in North America by Chronicle Books
680 Second Street
San Francisco, CA 94107

10   9   8   7

Quirk Books
215 Church Street
Philadelphia, PA 19106
www.quirkbooks.com

Contents

CHAPTER ONE: Get to Know Your Gnome 4

CHAPTER TWO: Gnome Lore 8

    Gnome Origin and Etymology 12

    The Gnome Experiment 14

CHAPTER THREE: Garden Gnomes 16

    The History of Lawn Ornaments 19

    The Oldest Living Garden Gnome 23

    Gnome Makers 26

    Garden Gnome Watching 101 27

CHAPTER FOUR: Gnomes in the Public Eye 32

    Gnome as Corporate Sponsor 33

    Gnome as Cult Figure 34

CHAPTER FIVE: Gnome Away from Home 38

    The Forces of Liberation 44

    The Gnome Manifesto 48

    Advice to New Gnomeowners 50

CHAPTER SIX: Your Gnome and You 52

    How to Create a Gnome Swing 57

    Maintaining Relations with Your Gnome 59

APPENDIX A: Where to Find Gnomes 62

APPENDIX B: Clubs, Organizations, and
    Clandestine Associations 63

About the Author 64

Credits 64

Avid collector Ron Bromsgrove with some of
his garden gnomes, London, England.

CHAPTER ONE

Get to Know Your Gnome

....

In European folklore, gnomes are believed to be household guardians or home spirits for both good and ill. They are friendly toward humans but also possess a sly charm and whimsy and are fond of practical jokes. Tradition holds that gnomes protect our precious belongings but are also notorious pranksters. If mistreated, they are reputed to torment humans with minor, but irritating, mischief like their distant cousins, the gremlins.

It is our sincere hope that the gnome within this kit brings you only good tidings. This tiny tome is intended as a guidebook for the new garden gnome owner. Within, we'll study the ways of the gnomenkind and provide you with tools to connect and communicate with these smug little garden dwellers. We'll also address some basic questions: What are gnomes? Where do they come from? And what connection does the garden statue have with the mythological being?

In part, this is a simple story about inanimate objects people place in their gardens. But there is another story here that deals with the thousands of people who animate their garden gnomes, dote on them, and, in extreme cases, physically interact with them. Some even believe garden gnomes spring to life when we aren't looking, sneaking into our bedrooms to steal our socks, gloves, earrings, keys, and underwear. (This may be one reason people keep their gnomes outside in the garden, as far away as possible from their underwear drawers.)

Establishing such a relationship with a statue requires a certain suspension of disbelief, and to seriously suggest that statues are alive, well, might qualify you for a trip to the neighborhood funny farm. But the practice does have a practical benefit. French anthropologist **Patrick Boumard,** who investigated the symbolic meaning of gnome statues in his work **Nains de Jardin,** wrote about the relationships people have with them: "I often found surprisingly strong affective connections. Some owners, for instance, wash their gnome every day. Others take their gnome in for the night and put him to bed. Many people talk to their gnome as if it were a favorite child. These objects allow a regression into childhood without a visit to the psychiatrist. I call them the 'Freud of the poor.'"

We might question the logic of this relationship and whether it can be valid if not reciprocated. Valid or not, for many this type of bond is desirable. After all, garden gnomes are patient interlocutors. They always listen. One can ask them questions and they never give stupid or impudent answers.

Good luck with yours.

A nineteenth-century illustration of a
"real" gnome from a Brothers Grimm story.

CHAPTER TWO

Gnome Lore

....

Much of the folklore concerning gnomes descends from northern Europe, chiefly **Scandinavia** and **Germany.** However, sects of gnomes have been reported across the planet; look-alike creatures exist in a variety of cultures.

In all cultures, gnomes are considered to be strange and mercurial little folk. They are keen thinkers and infamous tinkerers. They resemble little humans and have their own customs, talents, and supernatural abilities, many of which are quite extraordinary. It is said, for example, that when threatened by animals or humans, gnomes can transform themselves into mushrooms. They can become invisible at will, and only children with innocent eyes are able to see them. They are known to travel vast distances on the backs of wolves and on the wings of eagles. They have been seen jumping from treetops using dandelion seeds as parachutes.

The **Rosicrucians** (members of secret sects espousing religious mysticism in the seventeenth and eighteenth centuries) regarded gnomes as misshapen creatures, and many since have aligned them with trolls, goblins, and other undesirable denizens of the night. During the **Dark Ages,** it was believed that gnomes lived in the antechambers of the earth to guard its mineral resources. When humans began to dig mines, the gnomes were displaced. Many roamed the forests, building colonies in the root systems of giant trees. Others took up habitation with humans on farms and in gardens.

In Scandinavia it is customary to leave a bit of porridge or milk on the doorstep to appease the gnomes. If this offering is neglected, the gnomes become pesky and ill favor befalls the household. Norwegians refer to gnomes by various names: *Hudfolk* (hidden people), *Underjordiske* (underground dwellers), and the *Haugfolk* (people of the mounds). Folktales focus on a character named **"Nisse,"** an ambiguous and unpredictable trickster figure that secretly helps out with the farm chores and alternately, if mistreated, runs amuck and behaves like a poltergeist. The name Nisse is derived from **St. Nicholas,** and he is the Norwegians' jolly Saint Nick come Yuletide. (This is apparently the reason gnome statues resemble Santa Claus.) The Swedes have a similar version of the gnome named **Tomte,** meaning "homestead man."

In the old German tongue, gnomes were known as ***kubawalda*** (home administrators). German legend also depicts gnomes as farm helpers. The gnomes bunked in the barns and helped with gardening chores. They would secretly tend to the animals and clear cobwebs from corners of the barn. As a courtesy, the farmers would leave out beer, sausages, and buckets of water for the gnome women to wash their babies in.

In early accounts the relationship between humans and gnomes was a benevolent one. The gnomes were said to bring good luck and, in particular, to aid in the growth of vegetation. They were believed to infuse nutrients into the soil and capture the rays of celestial bodies in dew. Today this belief is embodied in the figure of the garden gnome. Many people who put gnome statues in their gardens aren't aware of these early superstitions, of course, but the garden gnome continues to work his Earth-magic, nevertheless.

For additional information concerning gnome habits and quirks, see **Wil Huygens's** seminal book *Gnomes* (1976). This modern-day classic depicts many characteristics of gnomenkind: their size, shape, life expectancy, social customs, sexual habits, and more. It is well-conceived, richly illustrated, and a good read for the serious gnome enthusiast.

Gnome Origin and Etymology

The origin of the word "gnome" isn't certain, but many hold that it was coined by the Swiss physician/alchemist **Paracelsus** (1493–1541), who referred to gnomes as earth spirits. In his theory, spirits personified the elements: gnomes (Earth), salamanders (fire), sylphs (air), and nymphs (water). He

One of the two thousand garden gnomes displayed
in the Bagatelle gardens in Paris, France, in 2000,
perhaps perusing a tome on etymology.

maintained that gnomes could breathe and move as freely through the Earth as birds through the air. Occasionally Paracelsus referred to them as pygmies or dwarfs, but also as **gnomi,** which etymologists believe comes from the Greek *genomoi* (Earth-dweller), or *gno-me* (thought, intelligence), or even *gnosis* (wisdom, knowledge). Taken together, these linguistic roots imply the earthly knowledge gnomes have inherited as their birthright.

The Gnome Experiment

Gnomes are humanoid; that is, they are derived from, but are not of, humankind. They have much in common with humans, as they do with the multitude of wood sprites that inhabit the forests of the world: pixies, elves, dwarfs, leprechauns, brownies, and the like. Gnomes are most often confused with dwarfs.

In his mystical text **A Book of Nymphs, Sylphs, Pygmies, and Salamanders, and Other Spirits** (1515), Paracelsus suggested that gnomes and other spirits descended from an alchemical ritual similar to one he had perfected to create a little humanoid he called a **"homunculus."** The process involved a convoluted recipe in which Paracelsus placed various herbs, silver and gold salts, tinctures, essences, bone shavings, skin fragments, blood, phlegm, and human semen in a sealed vial. The vial was then buried in a vat of horse manure and left for forty days to incubate and "magnetize." This would produce a little man who remained transparent until he had been nourished on human blood for forty days, at which point he became a fully formed little person.

Paracelsus writes of the meticulous recipe: "This procedure is of late known to me; it was, nevertheless, known to the wood-sprites and nymphs and giants long ago, because they themselves were sprung from the same source." It is doubtful whether Paracelsus actually discovered the recipe to make gnomes, but he did acknowledge them as real beings, and indeed, gnomes were believed to be real by many Europeans until the eighteenth-century **Enlightenment.**

An original gnome sculpture by Candice Kimmel, of the Kimmel company, a high-end garden gnome manufacturer in America.

CHAPTER THREE

Garden Gnomes

....

Wearing a colorful smock, leggings, sturdy boots, and a red conical hat that resembles a dunce cap, the garden gnome is poised for action. He stands sentinel in flowerbeds, frozen in a variety of poses with a shovel or hoe, pushing a wheelbarrow, fishing, or smoking a pipe. He leans against a toadstool or gazes across the frog pond. And always he grins. What can he be so giddy about? Scientists recently discovered that earthworms release **nitrous oxide** (laughing gas) into the environment. Could this be the cause? Obviously, he is pleased with the vegetable abundance around him and takes his duty as garden steward as a jocular pursuit—or so it would appear.

We see these perky, rosy-cheeked replicas as symbols of suburban contentment and high kitsch. And yet they provoke extreme reactions that inspire both reverence and contempt.

Take two extreme examples:

1. An Australian website titled "Die screaming with sharp things in your head" devotes itself to reproducing photographs of garden gnomes impaled by metal objects.

2. **The Gnome Reserve** in **Devonshire, England,** is home to more than one thousand gnome and pixie statues. Visitors may stroll the four acres of woodland streams, ponds, and gardens, viewing them in their natural habitat. The reserve loans guests gnome hats and fishing rods so they "don't embarrass the gnomes." *The Guinness Book of World Records* lists it as the largest garden gnome collection in the world. (See photo, overleaf.)

Some people actually have an irrational fear of garden gnomes stemming from *automatonophobia,* the fear of any inanimate object that resembles a sentient being. Perhaps the gnomes are too intent with their rigid eyes, disproportionate heads, and mischievous grins.

Those who find solace in their gardens find security in the fact that an elemental guardian keeps his eye trained on their vegetables. Yet others have a special fondness for their gnome figurines that can only be described as an obsession. They pamper him like a pet, wash him, rub his belly, and even frolic in the grass with him.

No matter what your attitude is toward the garden gnome—fear, worship, loathing, or even indifference—it is clear the gnome is here to stay.

The History of Lawn Ornaments

Historians date the concept of lawn ornamentation to Roman times, when noblemen set up altars to pagan gods in their gardens. The practice of personification or idolatry of statues has a clear religious origin. The devout Catholic worships a statue of the **Virgin Mary** because it represents her spirit. A statue of **Buddha,** whether serene or laughing, comes to embody the Buddhist tradition. The relic is venerated because

Ann Fawssett Atkin, founder of the Gnome Reserve in Devonshire, England, with a small portion of the reserve's collection.

of the link that unites it with a person and his or her faith. The gnome as symbolic statue guardian may have developed from its use in architecture during the **Middle Ages,** when gnomes were carved above doorways as a kind of benign anti-gargoyle.

During the **Renaissance** and **Baroque** periods, the fashion for garden sculpture spread northward from Italy, disseminated by Italian craftsmen and architects. Gardens throughout Europe were adorned with statuary: gods and goddesses, nymphs, satyrs, and various creatures both real and imaginary. At the height of the Baroque period, elaborate topiaries, mazes, and fountains became fashionable. The showpieces of this era are the elaborate garden designs at the palace at **Versailles, France,** where a set of statues depicting scenes from **Aesop's Fables** decorates the maze.

Gardens have always reflected societies' aesthetic, economic, and cultural tastes. In our own time, lawn decoration has been elevated to a new kind of art. Considered by some to be the ultimate transgression of taste, by others a unique means of personal expression, the act of animating the yard with inanimate objects is embedded in contemporary homesteading. Pink flamingos, lawn jockeys, clay frogs, porcelain deer, and mirror balls proudly populate the hovels of humankind. The garden gnome is the ancestor of these modern ornaments, and, for that honor, is considered to be the ultimate archetype of kitsch.

The Oldest Living Garden Gnome

The gnome statue is of recent origin. As a practice, its placement in the garden began in the late eighteenth century in a limited geographical area in the forests of **Thuringia** and northern **Bavaria** in Germany. One of the first and most famous accounts of garden gnomes dates to 1847, when **Sir Charles Isham** had twenty-one statuettes imported from Germany for his garden in **Northhamptonshire, England.** His neighbors deemed Isham an eccentric, and rumors circulated of midnight communions with his gnomes. He was a practicing **Spiritualist** and believed his gnomes were more than mere ornaments: they were alive and able to communicate with him.

For the next fifty years Isham crafted an elaborate shrine to the gnomes in his garden. He made labyrinthine crystal caves with tiny moats and fissures, planted miniature trees and shrubs, built subterranean tunnels and rooms, and in the midst of this otherworldly landscape arranged his gnomes in a large rockery.

After Isham's death, his daughters, who had harbored a dislike for the gnomes, had them all removed and purportedly destroyed—all except one, that is, which remained hidden in a crevice in the garden wall. One hundred and fifteen years later, the gnome was found and excavated (see photo, opposite). He was dubbed **"Lampy"** after the estate, **Lamport Hall.** Remarkably, the figure was well preserved and was named the oldest known garden gnome in the world. As reported by the BBC, little Lampy was insured for more than one million

Lampy, oldest known garden gnome,
pictured at his home at Lamport Hall in 2002.

pounds. Lampy was exhibited at gnome conventions around the world and, in 1993, was the first and only gnome ever admitted to the **Chelsea Flower Show.** Lampy now makes his permanent home on display at Lamport Hall.

Gnome Makers

The mass production of garden gnomes is attributed to two German craftsmen, **Philipp Griebel** and **August Heissner,** whose trademark ceramic gnomes first appeared in 1872. The **Heissner Company** still makes gnome statues, although they now specialize in hydraulics and garden accessories. Philipp's son took over the **Griebel Gnome** factory and his son after him. After a brief hiatus, great-grandson **Reinhard Griebel** revived the family tradition in 1987. The Griebel business closed in 2001, citing competition from less expensive plastic garden gnomes. Faced with bankruptcy, Griebel noted, "The garden gnome is a mirror of the German soul."

The Germans continue to be prolific producers and

collectors of garden gnomes. A certain national pride exists in Germany for domestic, handcrafted statues. In the 1990s many cheap, knock-off statues produced in neighboring countries to the east were smuggled into Germany. Several German companies filed and won copyright lawsuits on specific design features. The traditional manufacturers were able to persuade German border guards to seize illegal shipments and impose quotas on tourists transporting gnomes. The German border police tightened its security measures, and in 1997 it was reported that customs officials at the Czech border seized a shipment of eleven thousand gnomes. Since then, the copyright dispute has eased, and many imitation gnomes find their way into German gardens, much to the dismay of gnome purists.

Garden Gnome Watching 101

To the untrained eye, garden gnomes may appear rather similar: bearded, rosy-cheeked, wearing colorful outfits, and in good spirits. But if you spend a few moments to familiarize yourself with their features or field marks, you will recognize the subtle variations. Whether you are in the city or the field, you will be able to appreciate the nuances that differentiate one gnome from another and learn to identify them with the skill of an expert gnome watcher.

First take note of the material from which the gnome is made. Is it ceramic, plastic, concrete, or metal? Clay gnomes are considered to be classic and are often the most aesthetically pleasing. In addition, clay statues withstand the elements better than their plastic counterparts. Many ceramic gnomes are hand carved with fine attention to the particulars (wrinkles, teeth, thumbnails, etc.) and hand painted in choice colors.

clay gnome

Next note the gender. Garden gnomes are usually male, but female gnomes do exist. The women do not sport beards but display

female gnome

abundant bosoms. They are usually plump, wear traditional dresses, style their hair in pigtails, blush profusely, and don their own pointed caps, which are not red but instead green or sometimes blue. The females usually carry a bundle of wildflowers or a watering can.

Then take in the gnome's attire. The classic outfit for the male gnome is a frumpy green or blue shirt, brown pants, furry boots, and a red hat. However, there are many other styles of dress. They are seen in waistcoats, overalls, vests, tunics, aprons, and sometimes even bathing suits.

classically attired

For both sexes, the consistent features are bright colors, rosy cheeks, beaming smiles, and pointy hats. (One legend has it that the hat was originally a protective headgear for mine work. It functioned like an antenna to let gnomes know when to duck a beam.)

rosy-cheeked

Next turn your eye to the gnome's stance. Gnomes can be broadly categorized by the actions they perform and the objects they carry. In reality, they do nothing at all—the hard ceramic body gives little freedom of movement—but for the sake of comparison, let's say there are two basic categories: gnomes at leisure and those at work.

at leisure

Those at leisure carry fishing rods, accordions, flutes, walking sticks, pipes, or mugs of ale, or simply stand or recline on the lawn.

Those at work carry pickaxes, shovels, wheelbarrows, cords of wood, lanterns, or watering cans. Worker gnomes possess occupational skills, as well. There is the gardener, the angler, the miner, the carpenter, and the musician.

at work

Statue makers today have begun to

portray gnomes in more contemporary ways. Modern gnomes are often seen riding motor scooters, wearing headphones, carrying laptops, in beach chairs, without clothes, giving indecent gestures, or even talking on cell phones.

With an eye to the classes of material, gender, attire, and occupation, you can determine much about the intended purpose of the garden gnome. The gnomeowner most interested in inspiring Earth-magic will select a male worker gnome wearing a tunic and made of clay. A concrete or plastic gnome at leisure, of either gender and in any outfit, is a good indication of a novice gnomeowner. "Gnovelty" gnomes, including female gnomes, inebriates, and modernized gnomes, are typically owned by those celebrating the kitsch-value of the gnome and might be seen as a semi-mockery of the classic garden gnome.

"gnovelty" gnome

A bright-eyed gnome, photographed in 2002, makes it clear these statues are naturals for the limelight.

CHAPTER FOUR

Gnomes in the Public Eye

....

Garden gnomes are persistent symbols in our times. They appear in films, television programs, advertisements, songs, music videos, horror novels, and urban legends. There are gnome T-shirts, coffee mugs, and custom license plates. There are websites devoted to gnomes, and people spend hours in chat rooms discussing them. Gnomes have surfaced from the ancient depths of their subterranean grottoes to thrive and multiply in the public eye. In some respects, gnomes live larger now through the popularization of the statue than they ever did in fireside stories.

Gnome as Corporate Sponsor

Advertisers have exploited mythological creatures to endorse a variety of products. Elves sell cookies, giants hawk green beans, and genies sponsor cleaning products. Garden gnomes have been featured in commercials for **Polaroid** cameras, **Orkin** pest control, **Domino's** pizza, **Wherehouse** music, and **MSN** e-mail services. In 1997, director **Tim Burton** (*Beetlejuice, Planet of the Apes*) made his first television commercial about a gnome to sell chewing gum to the French. The commercial begins with a gnome frozen in a garden. As darkness falls, he comes to life, climbs over the garden wall, runs through the city, and hitches a ride on the back of a garbage truck into the forest where he bathes with a nude princess reminiscent of Snow White. The camera draws back to reveal a pack of **Hollywood** chewing gum (leaving the viewer to infer the connection).

Gnome as Cult Figure

Several gnomes have risen to prominence as pop icons. Typically nameless, credited simply as "the gnome," these few standouts have brought their entire brotherhood into the familiar glow of popular culture. Featured in numerous

This gnome painting hawks produce from its
barn-side home in LaConner, Washington.

television shows and films, they are usually cast as objects of endearment or as stolen property. A brief list of credits:

- *In the nineties sitcom* **Third Rock from the Sun,** *a garden gnome is one of the many pieces of kitsch in the apartment of the Solomon family (a group of aliens who take up residence on Earth). He is billed in the credits: "The Gnome—as himself."*

- *A garden gnome named "Squatsie" was featured in the sitcom* **Will and Grace** *as a memento from Will's childhood. In the episode "Went to a Garden Party," Will places Squatsie in his apartment's community garden. Grace comes over and is attacked by a wild bee. She swats at it with a shovel, but mistakenly smashes little Squatsie instead.*

- *In the British comedy* **The Full Monty** *(1997), the character Gerald is convinced to join a naked dance team by means of psychological warfare involving his prized collection of garden gnomes. At an important job interview, two of his friends hold up his gnomes outside the window, causing him to get distracted and lose the job.*

- *In* **Box of Moonlight** *(1997), a character called "The Kid" is a* *long-haired drifter who trades stolen garden gnomes and other lawn ornaments as his only source of income. In one scene he "borrows" a gnome from a yard in broad daylight while the owners stand in the doorway, incredulous.*

• *In* **Amelie** *(2001), a globetrotting garden gnome is featured in a subplot. The father of the title character is forlorn over his wife's death and takes solace in a dedicated obsession for his garden gnome. He longs to travel but cannot bring himself to leave home. Amelie steals the gnome and gives it to her stewardess friend. Photos of the gnome are sent from distant landmarks, and the bewildered father can only sigh at his gnome's adventures. In the end, the gnome returns home and the father gains the courage to travel himself.*

• *Disney is involved in a feature film entitled* **Gnomeo and Juliet.** *It is a tale of two star-crossed gnome statues—a female gnome kept inside and a male gnome kept in the garden. The gnomes are animated in 3D and set against a live background. Kate Winslet and Judy Dench voice the leads.*

Perhaps this gnome is thinking of home
from the beaches of Kauai, Hawaii.

CHAPTER FIVE

Gnome Away from Home

....

One of the earliest accounts of the **"Roaming Gnome"** prank comes from **Jan Harold Brunvand's** collection of urban legends *Curses! Broiled Again!* (1990). Brunvand describes how dozens of garden gnomes mysteriously disappeared from outside homes in Australia. They were discovered some months later in a forest in what an investigating officer described as a "nice arrangement." The statues were grouped around the largest of them, as if in secret council.

Stories about these "gnomads" have become a running joke. The scenario goes like this: During the night, the gnome vanishes from the garden. The owner assumes it to be stolen, but the statue has merely been kidnapped, borrowed for a time, and taken on a road trip. Instead of a ransom note, the owner receives a snapshot of the gnome from a distant landmark, say, the Eiffel Tower. On the back of the photo is a note that reads: "Went off to see the world—Love Paris—Wish you were here—your Gnome." Some weeks later another photo is sent from St. Petersburg and another from Bangkok. And then? In some cases the gnome returns home inexplicably one night with his beard smoothly pompadoured, a dark, lacquered suntan, sunglasses, and a little suitcase.

Most often the gnome is kidnapped, but sometimes it is swapped or appears in a random yard across town, much to the shock of the gnomeowner. The owner of the gnome is usually not amused. Neither are the police. (There is an interesting irony at work here because traditionally gnomes are the tricksters, deceivers, and in some cases, abductors of little children. In **Transylvania,** for example, the Roma people tell stories of an "earthman" they call **Pluvush,** who is rumored to steal infants in the night. Evidently, the gnomes are not the only ones fond of nocturnal hi-jinks.)

Liz Spera, president of the **International Gnome Club** in

Carmichael, California, comments, "You want to share your gnomes, but you really don't know if you want to put gnomes out in your front yard. People get attached to their gnomes. [Gnome theft] is a kind of cruel joke. There's a mean side to it."

Garden gnomes have found an advocate in **Fritz Friedmann,** who runs the **International Association for Protection of Garden Gnomes** from his apartment in Basel, Switzerland. He is a self-styled professor of nanology (the study of small things) and author of a book on gnomes titled ***Zipfel Auf*** (Hats Off). His organization has protected garden gnomes from criminality and abuse. Members are scarcely three hundred strong but organize gnome symposiums and exhibitions. They also publish a newsletter, ***The Garden Gnome Gazette.*** The association has grappled with important issues such as how tall gnomes can be (up to 68 cm) and whether female gnomes are acceptable in the garden (about which Friedmann has said, "It is unthinkable, completely unthinkable to mix in female gnomes with their male counterparts").

Some of the 101 garden gnomes recovered by French police after a mushroom hunter came upon them in a pine forest in Pondensac, France.

In February 2002, a gnome convention was held in the **Saxony** town of **Chemnitz,** featuring Friedmann as the keynote speaker. The group gathered to form a list of demands that included a mandate requiring a license to drive a lawnmower, an indictment against drunk lawnmower drivers, and a demand for better weather, more sunny days, and less acid rain to protect the gnomes who are exposed to the elements.

The Forces of Liberation

Some organizations push the **"Roaming Gnome"** idea to further extremes with a rallying cry for the emancipation of all garden gnomes. In their view, the gnomes are not being stolen but rather liberated from oppressive slave owners, freed from captivity, and returned to their natural woodland habitat. There is a clandestine international conspiracy behind these gnome-nappings, similar in scope and complexity to those organized to perform crop circle hoaxes and stage UFO sightings.

The coordinators of these fiendish pranks are known by many names: in English they are **"The Gnome Liberation Front,"** in Italian they are **"MALAG"** *(movimento autonomo per la liberazione delle anime giardino),* and in Swedish they are **"Tradgards-tomtarnas Befrielsefront."** These are but a few of the many hostile groups, loosely networked and sharing common goals.

There are conflicting reports as to when or where the movement began, but it is the French who take the pranks most seriously. During the 1990s, masked bandits infiltrated the sanctity of gardens across the Gallic countryside, anxious homeowners lost sleep, and police radios relayed bizarre schemes.

Many of the more dramatic incidents were claimed by **"Front de Liberation des Nains de Jardin" (FLNJ).** Drawing inspiration from the German Green Party, radical groups like the PLO and IRA, and their own tradition of bloody uprising, the French group has taken drastic steps to get its point across.

Casebook:

1996 Normandy, France. More than two hundred gnomes are found in a forest outside of the town of **Alencon.** The statues have been repainted, wear spectacles "to see in the dark," and are decorated with pasta "so they don't go hungry," according to FLNJ spokesmen.

1997 Bethunem, France. Three men are arrested and convicted of possession of 184 stolen gnomes and are given prison sentences of one to two months.

1998 Briey, Eastern France. Eleven gnomes dangle from a bridge by their necks. A suicide note is pinned to one of them. It reads, "When you read these few words, we will no longer be a part of your selfish world, which it has been our unhappy task to decorate."

2000 Paris, France. Twenty statues go missing from a gnome exhibition at the **Bagatelle** gardens. The FLNJ takes credit for the crime and demands, "This odious exhibition must be closed immediately. Or we will strike again!"

2001 Vosges, Saint-Die, and Chavelot, France. One hundred gnomes are discovered in a forest in **Vosges** region. The next day seventy-four gnomes are arranged on the steps of a cathedral in **Saint-Die.** FLNJ literature stated the mission was to "de-ridiculize the figures." In **Chavelot** dozens of gnomes and other items are arranged in a traffic roundabout to spell out the words "FREE THE GNOMES." Police treat the actions seriously because, as one spokesman commented, "Many people, especially the elderly, are actually very attached to their garden gnomes."

2001 Minimum number of garden gnomes relocated to the forest since 1996 by the FLNJ: 6,000. (*Harpers Index*, October 2001)

One can imagine the chaos when the French police reunite the recovered gnomes with their owners. Do all the owners gather around in the station parking lot, sort through the pile of colored figures, and finally say: "There! That one is mine!

That's little Smokey"? In one report from the newspaper **Sud Ouest,** the local police chief requested that people bring photographs of their gnomes to back up their claims.

The Gnome Manifesto

Gnome liberators usually leave a leaflet, banner, or hastily scrawled note at the scene of the crime with a list of demands. One sample from a liberation manifesto reads: "How long, fellow gnomes, how long have we listened to the smooth whispers of the man-species as they pick among our friends at the local garden center, praising one, rejecting another?"

But what is the true mission of these organizations? Groups like the FLNJ demand the liberation of garden gnomes for a two-fold purpose:

1. To return the gnomes to their natural habitat (the forest presumably).

2. To rid the urban environment of tacky kitsch that defames ancient myths.

Rock City Gardens, a nature reserve in Chattanooga, Tennessee, is just one of many organizations that house worker garden gnomes.

The general consensus or modus operandi is to free the gnomes from captivity in a world of strip malls and asphalt roads. Liberationists believe gnomes have been disenfranchised, subjected to cruel torture, enslaved to do gardeners' work, forced to smile and wield pickaxes in the cold rain and snow, the targets of children's jokes, bird droppings, and the unwitting recipients of dogs lifting their legs.

Advice to New Gnomeowners

The traveling gnome idea, clever as it is, has inspired scores of similar copycat pranks with slight variations. There is a cultural expectation of the event, and as a gnomeowner, you must prepare for your gnome to go on holiday at some point. No garden, however small, is safe from gnome thieves.

There are a few precautions gnomeowners can take to ensure their little object of adoration doesn't get hijacked. If the gnome is outside in the garden, a basic precaution is to set the feet in cement. For more security, rebar shafts can be used to brace its legs. An alarm system can be installed with motion detectors and floodlights. An elaborate cage could be constructed around the gnome with cut-glass wire. Alternatively, there is the option of bringing the gnome inside for the night—a compromise, to be sure, since then the underwear drawer becomes an open target for gnome mischief.

If the gnome is kept at the office, it can be rubber cemented to the desktop. A defense system could be rigged with an alarm clock and booby traps of binder clips and rubber bands. The owner also has the option of stowing the gnome in a file cabinet at night—a risky move, as he or she may return to discover the files mysteriously shifted during the night.

You may choose to use your new gnome for a variety of tasks,
such as acting as a paperweight or guarding your stapler.

Your Gnome and You

....

A gnome statue is a totem. It embodies the spirit of the Earth and is traditionally kept to watch over the garden or protect an entryway. If you keep your garden gnome at the office or other similar location, you must create an environment that suits his special abilities.

The traditional place for a gnome statue is outdoors. Depending on where the statue is positioned, it is referred to as either a garden gnome or a lawn gnome. Included in your kit is a wee bit of lawn to place your gnome upon so that its connection with the Earth is firmly preserved. Gnomes like to be surrounded by plants and vegetation. Accordingly, this kit also contains three flowers that can be positioned around your gnome to create both a healthy space for the gnome and a visually enticing garden.

Also included is an assortment of backdrops with which to create a diorama. Gnomes are prolific travelers. You can position the gnome so he blends seamlessly into the realistic environs of Paris, suburban America, the Matterhorn in Switzerland, or his own garden home.

Step One: *Remove lawn from package and place in desired location. Desktops, windowsills, and countertops work well, but any hard, flat surface will do.*

Step Two: *Remove gnome from package. Place him where it feels right.*

Step Three: *Remove flowers from package and stick the stems into the lawn so that flowers stand upright.*

Step Four: *Remove backdrops from package. Select desired location and return the other card to the box. The backdrop should be inserted into the slot between the edge of the turf and its frame so that the gnome faces away from it and toward you.*

Step One

Step Two

Step Three

Step Four

As you get to know your gnome, you might want to find him some kin. When displayed together, a group of gnome statues can have a powerful visual effect. If you found a medium-sized gnome, a large gnome, and then an even larger one, you could line them up in a row like some kind of inside-out nesting doll. You might forge a community for your gnome and surround him with a menagerie of miniscule counterparts; action figures, Thumbelina figurines, worry dolls, Trolls, Lego characters, bobble-heads, wind-up animals, plastic dinosaurs, small bowling trophies, bronze replicas of world landmarks, and the like would all complement your gnome, and when viewed together would create a stunning tableau.

Some kind of shrine might be constructed around your gnome with tinsel, candy wrappers, coins, and other glittery objects. You could leave your gnome offerings of bird feathers, lint, a locket of hair, and other fetishes. Like the porridge left on doorsteps by Scandinavians, these totems will ensure that the gnomes are happy and will resist the urge to stir up mischief. Remember, when Gnomes are happy they are beneficent spirits who steer good luck your way.

How to Create a Gnome Swing

It is generally agreed that the happiest gnome in the garden is the swinging gnome. Gnomes love nothing more than to feel the wind whistling through their long white beards as they swing. To help your gnome acclimate to his new home, you can build a little swing from a length of paper clips, binder clips, and a memo pad and suspend him from your desk or cubicle wall.

Step One: *Create the chains. Link together three two-inch paper clips end to end. You will need two of these chains.*

Step Two: *Each chain should be linked to a binder clip. Thread the chain through the top lever and link it to the bottom lever.*

Step Three: *Clip each binder clip onto either end of a small sticky note pad.*

Step Four: *Hang swing from two thumbtacks on a bulletin board.*

Step Five: *Place gnome on note pad and allow the breeze to set him*

Step One

Step Four

Step Two

Step Three

Step Five

swinging. (You may want to secure gnome to pad with a small piece of double-stick tape.)

These are but a few suggestions. We leave it to you to imagine other ways to occupy your garden gnome. If your intent is to use the gnome to bring good luck, remember he isn't a rabbit's foot or genie's lamp (although you may consider rubbing his belly or stroking his beard), nor is he like the Blarney Stone or a fairy tale toad that can be kissed for luck. No, the best way to acknowledge your gnome is with a simple smile, a few kind words, or a solemn, respectful nod of the head.

Maintaining Relations with Your Gnome

Assuming that you will keep your gnome around the house or office, erasers, staplers, or scissors might all be susceptible to the gnome's mischief. To prevent this pilferage, take care to keep your little fellow happy. Give him a name (you might consider choosing a name reflecting the German or Scandinavian roots of gnome lore, perhaps Jan or Olaf);

acknowledge him when you sit at your desk in the morning; and seek out his wisdom on key matters.

Gnomes are industrious creatures. The garden variety is often seen at work, pushing wheelbarrows or digging up mushrooms. When not working he is at leisure with his fishing rod or flute. Give your gnome something to do on your desk. If nothing else, give him a pipe to smoke. Pretend that you are a pint-sized statue with a reputation for Earth-magic—what sort of tools would you require? Perhaps a slingshot fashioned from a rubber band and a thumbtack, or an axe constructed from a pencil and an X-acto knife blade.

Gnomes like to feel useful—idleness is the root of gnome mischief. Think of useful tasks the gnome might perform; for example, if you have a difficult itch on your back, you could use the gnome's pointy hat to scratch it, or he might be used to stand guard over important documents. These simple duties will ensure a beneficial and trouble-free coexistence with your garden gnome.

You should be patient when communicating with your gnome. Above all, treat him with kindness and respect. Gnomes have long acted as wise accomplices to humans. They are notoriously difficult to manage, but when their confidence is won they are faithful and true companions.

Most importantly, gnomeowners shouldn't feel self-conscious about displaying their gnomes in public. They should do so proudly. Gnomes have always raised the eyebrows of neighbors, postmen, and friends. In the end, who is to say how you should decorate your own space? Be secure in the knowledge that you have a sentinel to watch over your work.

More than a mere statue, even more than a keepsake or a piece of kitsch, your gnome is a rare being.

Enjoy him.

Appendix A: Where to Find Gnomes

If you're unable, ethically or physically, to steal a gnome, you can always take the more acceptable route and buy one from a vendor.

The Internet has become a vast storehouse for the gnome connoisseur, and there is a wide variety of styles to choose from. If you are searching for high quality ceramic statues, the Kimmel Co., operating out of the United States, markets fine models created by its founder.

Internet vendors of garden gnomes:

Crocus www.crocus.co.uk

Deutsches Haus www.deutscheshaus.cc

Garden Gnomes Need Homes www.garden-gnomes-need-homes.com

The Gnome Shop www.thegnomeshop.com

Gnomerama Limited www.gnomerama.com

Kimmel Gnomes www.kimmelgnomes.com

Knot Hole Station www.knotholestation.com

Krupps www.krupps.com

The Magic Forest www.themagicforest.com

P.W. Westimex www.westimex.com.pl

Ray-Mar Gnomes www.outdoorgnomes.com

Zwergenpower www.zwergenpower.com

Appendix B: Clubs, Organizations, and Clandestine Associations

Gnome Protectors:

The Gnome Reserve. West Putford, Nr Bradworthy, N Devon, EX22 7XE England. Tel. 0870 845 9012. www.gnomereserve.co.uk

International Association for Protection of Garden Gnomes. c/o Fritz Friedmann, Sekretariat IVZ56, St. Jakobstrasse 103, CH-4052 Basel, Switzerland. www.zipfelauf.com

International Gnome Club. c/o Liz Spera, The International Gnome Club, 6740 Duncan Lane, Carmichael, CA, 95608-2817, USA. Tel. (916) 944-2741. GNOMENET@aol.com

International Gnome Day (June 21). Organized by Beryl the Gnome. www.beryl-the-gnome.co.uk

Gnome Liberators:

Front de Liberation des Nains de Jardin (FLNJ). www.flnjfrance.fr.st

Gnome Liberation Army. www.gnome-liberation-army.co.uk

Mouvement Terroriste pour la Liberation des Nains de Jardin (MTLNJ). www.mtlnj.cjb.net

Movimento Armato per la Liberazione delle Anime de Giardino (MALAG). www.malag.it, info.malag@libero.it

About the Author

Marcus B. Mennes lives aboard a houseboat in Seattle, Washington. There is a small garden at the marina where his gnome "Pheromone" keeps an eye on things.

Credits